DIGGING FOR DINOSAURS

Haydn Middleton

G000122305

CONTENTS

DISCOVERING THE LOST WORLD

Dinosaurs died out millions of years ago, but they once lived all over the world. There were no people on Earth at the time of the dinosaurs, so how do we know dinosaurs once lived here?

▶ **This never happened! Dinosaurs died out millions of years before people started living on earth.**

Today, many people are fascinated by dinosaurs. They want to find out what dinosaurs looked like, how they moved, how they behaved and how they lived. Some people study dinosaurs for a living. These people are called **palaeontologists** (say 'pally-on-tollo-jists').

DIGGING UP THE PAST

When dinosaurs died, their bodies became covered in mud, earth or sand. Dinosaur skin, bones, teeth, eggs and even dinosaur dung were buried under layers of soil and rock. Some dinosaur parts rotted away, but some were **preserved**. After millions of years, these preserved parts hardened into **fossils**.

Palaeontologists dig up dinosaur fossils and study them. They use the fossils to piece together the puzzle of the dinosaurs. They develop **theories** about what dinosaurs looked like, how they moved, what they ate ... and what killed them.

Palaeontologists at work

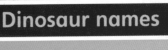

Dinosaur names

The word 'dinosaur' is Greek. It means 'terrible lizard'. Palaeontologists make up names for each new type of dinosaur they find. The first dinosaur discovered was called Megalosaurus (say 'mega-low-saw-rus') which means 'big lizard'.

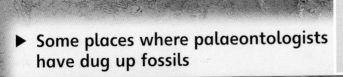

▶ Some places where palaeontologists have dug up fossils

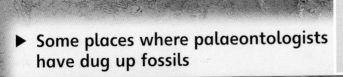

Arctic Ocean

NORTH
AMERICA

EUROPE

ASIA

Atlantic
Ocean

Pacific Ocean

AFRICA

SOUTH
AMERICA

Indian
Ocean

AUSTRALASIA

Southern Ocean

STONE BONE SKELETONS

A hundred years ago in Africa, some palaeontologists found a place where many dinosaurs had died. They dug up thousands of fossil bones there.

The palaeontologists began to piece together the bones – it was a bit like a huge jigsaw puzzle! They carefully worked out how the bones fitted together and eventually they constructed an entire dinosaur **skeleton**.

Thousands of dinosaur bones were uncovered at this site in Africa.

The palaeontologists learned a lot from the dinosaur skeleton. It showed them the dinosaur's shape, and gave them an idea of what the dinosaur might have looked like when it was alive.

By studying the dinosaur's teeth, the palaeontologists worked out that the dinosaur was a plant eater. Its teeth were flat and rough, and not sharp enough for chewing meat.

▶ **This is the Brachiosaurus skeleton in a museum.**

The dinosaur also had a very long neck, which made the palaeontologists believe that it ate leaves from the high treetops.

The palaeontologists called the dinosaur a Brachiosaurus (say 'brack-ee-oh-saw-rus').

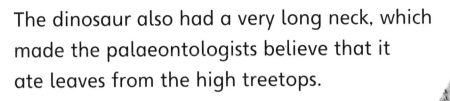

This is what palaeontologists think a Brachiosaurus looked like. It could have weighed up to 80 tonnes – as heavy as 13 elephants!

MONSTER MEAL

Most dinosaurs ate plants, but some dinosaurs were **carnivorous**. That means they ate other dinosaurs.

The Coelophysis (say 'seel-uh-fy-sis') was only 3 metres long, but it was a ferocious carnivore.

The Coelophysis moved quickly on two legs. It used its sharp claws to grab and tear apart other dinosaurs.

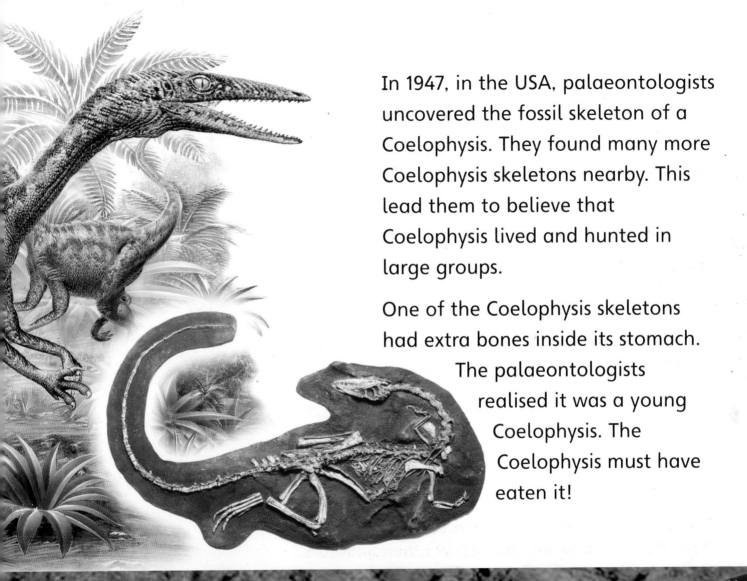

In 1947, in the USA, palaeontologists uncovered the fossil skeleton of a Coelophysis. They found many more Coelophysis skeletons nearby. This lead them to believe that Coelophysis lived and hunted in large groups.

One of the Coelophysis skeletons had extra bones inside its stomach. The palaeontologists realised it was a young Coelophysis. The Coelophysis must have eaten it!

FOSSIL FEATHERS

Most dinosaurs lived on the ground, but some small dinosaurs could climb trees. One tree-dwelling dinosaur was called a Microraptor (say 'my-crow-rap-tor').

It was about 1 metre long and had curved claws to help it grip the tree trunk and branches.

EARLY BIRDS

This squirrel cannot fly, but its large flaps of skin help it to glide through the air, as the Microraptor may once have done.

The Microraptor had feathers on its arms, legs and tail. Palaeontologists know that the Microraptor could not fly, because its skeleton shows it had no wings. But they think that this dinosaur used its feathers to help it **glide** as it jumped from tree to tree.

One theory is that, over thousands of years, the feathered arms and legs of these dinosaurs gradually **evolved** into wings. These dinosaurs became the first birds.

DINOSAUR JIGSAWS

Most palaeontologists do not find whole skeletons. More often than not, all they find is a few fossil bones. It is like finding just a few pieces of a dinosaur jigsaw. Palaeontologists study each fossil carefully and work out which dinosaur the bones once belonged to and what the dinosaur might have looked like.

▼ This is what palaeontologists think Baryonyx walkeri looked like.

BILL'S JIGSAW CLAW

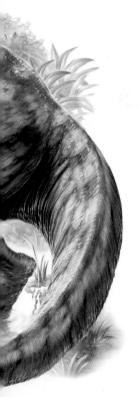

Bill Walker wasn't a palaeontologist, but he loved digging up fossils as a hobby. Near London in 1982 he dug up a huge fossil claw. Palaeontologists then dug deeper at the same spot and found more fossils, but they didn't recognise the dinosaur that the bones came from. Bill Walker had discovered an entirely new type of dinosaur!

The palaeontologists called this new dinosaur Baryonyx walkeri (say 'ba-ree-on-ix wal-ker-ee'). Baryonyx means 'heavy claw', and walkeri just means Bill Walker found it. They named the dinosaur after Bill!

HOW DID DINOSAURS WALK?

As dinosaurs roamed the land they made footprints in the mud. Some of these footprints dried out, grew hard and later became fossils. Palaeontologists study fossil footprints to work out what kind of dinosaur made them and how it moved.

Some dinosaurs walked on four legs; others walked upright on their hind legs. Upright dinosaurs usually had tails that dragged along the ground and left tracks behind the footprints. Four-legged dinosaurs held their tails off the ground when they walked.

Palaeontologists used to think that the Iguanodon (say 'ig-warr-no-don') walked on two legs, until they noticed there were no tail tracks near its footprints. This showed that Iguanodon must have walked on four legs.

GREAT DINOSAUR MISTAKES

Palaeontologists don't always get things right. About 200 years ago, in England, a palaeontologist found some Iguanodon fossils. There were lots of fossil bones, including a mysterious fossil spike.

The palaeontologist decided that the spike was a horn on the dinosaur's head. Years later, other palaeontologists dug up a whole Iguanodon skeleton and discovered that the dinosaur had spikes attached to each front foot. The first theory had been wrong.

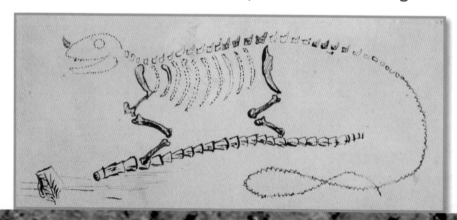

◀ Early drawings of the Iguanodon show a spike on the dinosaur's head.

TAKE A GUESS

These fossil arms are 2.4 metres long, and the claws are 26 centimetres long. They belong to a huge dinosaur called Deinocheirus (say 'dy-no-kee-rus'). Palaeontologists think the dinosaur looked like this, but they cannot be sure because no other bits of this dinosaur have been found. Sometimes palaeontologists just have to guess what a dinosaur looked like from the bits they find.

THE END OF THE DINOSAURS

Dinosaurs are now extinct – this means that they no longer exist.

All dinosaur fossils are at least 65 million years old and some are much, much older. But the last of the dinosaurs finally died out about 65 million years ago.

Palaeontologists have many theories about why this happened, but no one really knows because it was such a long time ago. What killed the dinosaurs is one of the greatest unsolved dinosaur mysteries!

GLOBAL WARMING

One theory is that the Earth gradually became much hotter. The dinosaurs couldn't live in these extreme temperatures and slowly died out.

GLOBAL FREEZING

Another theory is that the planet became much colder and in some regions froze completely. The dinosaurs then died because they couldn't survive in such cold weather.

Neither of these theories, however, explains why the dinosaurs disappeared so quickly. Many palaeontologists believe that something much more dramatic happened ...

THE METEORITE THEORY

Meteorites (say 'mee-tee-or-rites') are lumps of rock that exist in outer space. They can be as small as a pebble or as large as a mountain. Occasionally these meteorites collide with planet Earth. The small ones are harmless, but about 65 million years ago a giant meteorite hit the Earth in the region that is now Mexico. Even now there is still a huge hole in the ground where the meteorite fell. It must have been enormous!

This is where the meteorite hit Mexico. The hole is more than 300 kilometres wide. Some of it is now covered with jungle and some of it is under the sea.

Here is the palaeontologists' theory:

The giant meteorite crashed into Earth and shook the whole planet.

It filled the sky with rocks and dust that may have blocked out the sunlight for many years.

Without sunlight, the world's plants died.

Without food, the plant-eating dinosaurs died.

Without other dinosaurs to eat, the meat-eating dinosaurs died.

GLOSSARY

carnivorous   meat-eating

evolved   changed over time

fossils   bits of bone and other body parts that have been **preserved** over time

glide   sail through the air with wings that do not move

meteorite   a rock that falls to earth from space

palaeontologist   someone who digs up fossils and studies dinosaurs

preserved   kept whole or safe

skeleton   all of the bones of a body joined together

theories   ideas about things that cannot be known for sure